9 HORRIBLE MISTAKES THAT COST DEALERS & FABRICATORS CRORES IN WPC INDUSTRY

ANKUR HORA

FOUNDER OF INDIA'S FASTEST GROWING
WPC COMPANY

Worldwide Publishing by

PENDOWN PRESS
Powered by **Gullybaba Publishing House Pvt. Ltd.,**
An ISO 9001 & ISO 14001 Certified Co.,
Regd. Office: 2525/193, 1st Floor, Onkar Nagar-A, Tri Nagar,
Delhi-110035
Ph.: 09350849407, 09312235086
E-mail: info@pendownpress.com
Branch Office: 1A/2A, 20, Hari Sadan, Ansari Road,
Daryaganj, New Delhi–110002
Ph.: 011-45794768
Website: PendownPress.com

First Edition: 2022
ISBN: 978-93-5554-153-6

Layout and Cover Designed by Pendown Graphics Team

Dedicated to...

My Dealers & Fabricators, who have given me Immense learning on this journey of success in the last one decade & my Mentors who Gave me Direction to Execute this Book.

Contents

Let's Begin

Termite. Borer, Dampness, Construction Delays, Swelling, Delamination, Warping, Non-Engineered Product, VOC Emissions, Non Green Products, Fake Water Proof & Many More.

These Words Were So Commonly Painful for every stakeholder doing construction at any level using Conventional products.......Their pain was so Aggregated that they All Needed Solutions for the same in many Interior & exterior Applications a decade ago.

Ecoste WPC invented the Products which solved all These Problem in Majorly all their Applications Like:

- Door Opening Solution
- Furniture Solution
- Kitchen Solution
- Shaft covering Solutions

These all Applications Substituting the conventional product really helped Below stakeholders Across Country to;

500+ Successful Government Projects Across Nation Completed With Zero Delay & Zero Defect

1500+ Multistory Private Projects Completed with 100% Satisfaction

- Complete Project Prior Timelines
- Build Green Structures
- Reduce Cost in Long Run
- Create Maintenance Free Structures

Not Just this, our solutions also helped More than 1 Lac + independent houses in last one decade to solve the Problem we are working at...

The WPC Product line has become a choice of every Private Group Housing builder to Every Government engineer. The Industry has grown from 100 Crore to 3000 Crore Per Annum in just 10 years. It is estimated that the WPC market size will be more than 1 Billion i.e 8000 Cr by 2025.

The dealers who have been associated with us for last one decade have taken great competitive advantage. This is majorly due to our distinct marketing initiatives, educating customers through our videos, excellent standardised quality product.

We have so many success stories across the country of our dealers & fabricators who are making 3-10 Lacs of Monthly Profit working with us....They are ready to take their game to the next level as in our 10 year of operation, we are setting up India's Largest Italian State of the Art WPC Manufacturing Facility

This will Provide 15000 Metric Tonnes of Italian quality WPC which will help the Dealers to Get the WPC with High Fiber content at lesser cost & get the delivery in less than 7 Days.

If you are thinking Is this book worth a read for me or not...then go through the introduction chapter, which will give you clarity on how it will benefit you.

Acknowledgements

First and foremost, I would like to thank my parents, My Wife Aastha & My daughter Vedikka & Son Vivann who have been a Source of Inspiration.

I also want to thank Mr. V.M Upadhyay Ji for his Direction & ongoing guidance.

I would also like to thank my Marketing Mentor Akshar ji who has Inspired me to create Immense Value for My Customer.

I am thankful to My Friend Dinesh Verma, CEO, Pendown Press and his team for their support and suggestions throughout the creative process.

Chapter 1

Is it for Me?

I do not claim to be a Sales Guru or Marketing Genius... However, I do want to share my experience of close to a decade of being in the Building Material, especially the Wood Polymer composite i.e WPC industry.

Each page is intentionally written to Cut the Crap (No B.S.) to make your journey to Lead and not compete even if you are new to WPC or working with other Brands in the industry.

You must be thinking: why should I invest hours in reading this Book?...And why should I listen to your Suggestions | Advice mentioned in the Book...WHY?

If indeed you are thinking all these... Let me ask you a question.

Are you really ambitious to start and grow your business using WPC solutions as a vehicle?

If you are new or already selling WPC, are you ready to lead and dominate in your Market?

If the answer to the first question is YES and the answer to the second question is... LEAD.... (Not Compete), I assure you that this investment of a few hours will make you proud of yourself for the rest of your life.

If the answer is NO to the first question, then surely you must not go ahead as we really want to make your research cheaper, better and faster.

If you are wondering who will get the best value from this Book, here's the answer:

- If you are new to the building material industry and planning to venture into the WPC Industry, this is going to be a truly insightful journey for you....
- If you are already in the building material construction industry and planning to add the WPC Solution to your kitty, then surely it will save you a lot of time and let you stay away from massive physical and mental pain...

If you are wondering: who will get the best value from this Book, here's the answer:

- If you are already selling WPC Solutions, and feel that you are struggling to find customers or you've to sell at your customer's asking price or the market is too competitive. then...it's a MUST READ for you since it will showcase many success stories that are dominating in this industry.

These success stories will give you deep insights into a step-by-step pathway to lead in your territory...and it will also make you aware of the important steps you bypassed which you must have known in advance....

This book will help you even if you are feeling overwhelmed by thinking of any or a few of the feelings listed below...

Go through these...

- I am a Newbie in this big emerging industry.
- I don't come from a Sales and Marketing background.
- I don't have a strong customer base for selling this solution
- Is this industry the right fit for me and will I be able to succeed in it?
- Whether I will be able to craft a Long-Term future in this Industry or not?

HOLD...Thamba....

Just try to think... What would have been in the mind of the Director before creating the EPIC Movie ***Bahubali?***...

His Left Brain must have been analysing whether would it be possible to make this epic? Would it generate sufficient ROI?

While the right brain would have been popping 100's of images of the sets where it could be executed.

Thus, if these above objections popping in your head are increasing your nostalgia and letting you scratch your head out of confusion....then let me make you FIRM about one thing that this Book is structured in a beautiful way. It will surely help you speed your pace on this learning graph in this industry. This will help even if you are in this industry selling any building product for 10, 20 or 30 years or even more...

WHY... If you are thinking that now you will tell me know how to work in my dealership business when I have done that for years...

This comes from your EGO and my only request to you is to drop your e egoistic thoughts...Because if you won't drop this thought that means you aren't coachable...Think in this way that your mind is a painting canvas...The old story is painted over it in the form of painting....Now,the 2 options that you have is to either stay with your old story... or, drop the old canvas and be ready to put over the new canvas....be ready to build a new story...

The whole book is structured in such a way that first you will be getting access to 12 mistakes which you may make while entering in the WPC Industry. Once your awareness is increased to a level that you learn from the mistakes which I have observed others making in last 9 Years. You are surely going to get some AHA moments while reading the same.

Once you bypass these mistakes in the beginning and avoid the mental and physical pain you would have undergone by doing and learning from your actions. Then thereafter, you will raise the curtain on how to lead selling quality WPC solution in the long run...

Since this book is written for you to get maximum value, then I want you to take maximum value...This will be only possible, if we communicate...yes...HOW?

Don't worry...I want you to give your 1000% while reading this book and treat it as a manual as I will be asking you several questions at different intervals..Whenever,you see a question...pause and write your answer there and then using a pencil.

There and then...I will do it later Na...NO...if you are really serious about the game you gonna start to play,then doing it wholeheartedly is always better than doing it with hole in the heart...BUT before it....let me express what I have in my heart for you.

From my heart to your heart and from my soul to your soul,I really want to Thank You for your time and efforts, and abundance of gratitude. Let's begin with the mistakes which cost you crores in the WPC industry.

Chapter 2

Entering in Industry without the Prior Market Research

Let's listen to the answers I get to the questions that I ask over calls...You will start feeling some sense out of it. You will feel...(A haaa)...

Ankur (Asking to New Prospect to WPC): What is motivating you to enter this Industry?

Answer: I have seen some videos of yours on Youtube or heard of WPC products in my area, so I thought it's a good product to work upon.

Some of them say that I have researched that it's a good product, solves problems of termite, borer, dampness ....and being a green product, it seems like a futuristic product.

One Said, I am searching for a new dealership opportunity in selling any good product, so, I feel WPC will do justice with it.

Ankur (Already in WPC) : What has motivated you to get in touch with us?

One Said, I am working with branded WPC Product, but not satisfied with quality and looking for a better quality product.

Some say, delay in supplies in WPC from plants results in loss of orders and Revenue.

Majority say, looking forward to a company where we can get all the WPC solutions with one company.

Few say, for more profits, we are searching for a New WPC Vendor.

Let me flashback your scene of how I entered this Industry., It was a pain in my heart and determination in my head to find a solution to the problem for my country. I remember very clearly that I wanted to make every house (Project) free from the risk of termites, borer and dampness.

Your mind might say that isn't it same to call the two of the points mentioned below :

I want to enter the industry because the product is termite | Water Proof... **OR**

I wanted to make every house (Project) to live free from the risk of termites, borer and dampness.

These 2 Statements have a hell lot of difference...It might sound the same, but there is a huge difference in the context of both the statements.

Thus, I would like to ask if you are new to WPC or already in WPC. What's your WHY to enter the WPC industry?

Listening to this one word WHY may not make that much deep sense. However, let me share a powerful distinction which one of my mentors shared with me. It says.....

The bigger the WHY, the Easier the HOW

Thus, what I would like to share with you is that understanding/ your WHY to enter the WPC industry or choosing a new company in WPC industry. Both do require a strong market research prior to entering the industry.

A strong market research....You might ask yourself now how to do market research...What elements to cover and whom to consult?

The elements which you need to do the market research would be

1. What is the market size of the WPC in Your territory?
2. What product works in your territory?
3. Who is your customer base and how does your ideal client look?
4. What is the main problem which your customer is trying to solve?
5. What are the payment terms on which the different customer categories work?
6. What is the quantum which different types of customer categories Procures?
7. What is the average order size in different customer categories?

8. What is the inventory which you should hold and maintain?
9. What is the baseline pricing which is running in the market?
10. What is the difference in the organized and unorganized sector?
11. What is the price difference between organized and unorganized players?
12. What marketing would be required to get the right prospect leads and in what volume?
13. What is the most relevant application for each product solution in WPC running in your territory?
14. What is the medium to generate the leads and at what cost?
15. What is the percentage of the customer base which just takes the material or takes the material with complete installation only?

If you are thinking on how to answer these questions and how to begin my market research. Whom should I Call first or visit first....then THAMBA

Chapter 3

Less Clarity on Product Line to begin with...

This mistake, if you understand, will surely help you to make your game plan unshakable. After working with 100s of dealers and speaking to 1000s of Prospects in the last one decade, I learnt something significant.

I remember when I spoke to the majority of the prospects and asked them a single question

What product line would you like to start with?

Few used to say: All

Some Replied: Can start with the products you recommend Ankur ji.

Being authentic a few years ago , my answer used to be "Start with all products as you don't know what customers may ask. Start with all Products."

However, slowly I got mature understanding the market dynamics with the continuous feedback of my dealer, I learnt a million-dollar learning for those who want to get into the WPC Industry.

Product being the core thing, you have to understand that every product solves a problem. The problem is unique. Let me give you an example.

2 days ago, my dad got a fan and got it installed replacing the existing one..I asked him if his fan was working fine, then, why did he change it?

His answer was because I saw it online and I really liked it...

What's special about it other than the fancy new design?

He handed over me the remote...and said it works with remote and has an in built light also.

I said...That's crazy. But, nothing special in it. ...Isn't it?

He said the main reason isn't this...The 2 main reasons are that its airflow doesn't hit hard and is very smooth and second reason is that, it understands the body and room temperature and controls the fan speed accordingly and keep it regulating.

After listening to this, I understood. it solves a problem of a consumer that he doesn't have to disturb his sleep to control the regulator.

I mean it reduces the physical and mental pain or effort of the user...Why won't anyone mind spending 4 times for a fan too....?

Hope this example gave you clarity that WHY people buy....and how much solving acore problem of a consumer is important.

Thus, I would like to recommend that selecting to right product line in the beginning is very important to accelerate fast. The biggest mistake that Dealers or even OEMs Make is to see what others are selling and model that pls. dont do that. If you are this that and feel that the sales are struggling, it is time to calibrate the product choice that you made.

What happens when you make a choice seeing others is that you miss The customer category you have or want to cater To....let me explain with examples.

A UPVC fabricator choosing all products to start instead first choosing door opening solution ONLY.

A modular furniture choosing all products instead of choosing sheets for kitchens. Getting confidence and then moving to next application in fact..

A timber merchant choosing all products instead Just choosing door frame and window frame solution.

A dealer of panel product choosing all products rather than first choosing sheets for kitchens, wardrobes, paneling and furniture.

You must be thinking that why are you emphasizing on "One Solution One Application."

I would like to explain it by using an example which My mentor taught that common in these 3 cricketers:

1. Ms Dhoni
2. Adam Gillchrist
3. K L Rahul

The common thing is that by doing wicket keeping they understood the reflexes and that made him a good batsman too...because they could understand slowly both the sides of the game. I learnt 2 Lessons from this.

First learning is: patience is the jewel of a Businessman | Entrepreneur

Second is that in cricket you learn, **Ball By Ball,** in sales you learn **Call by Call,** in product you Learn Application by Application.

Every time, you do an application, you will have new learning...

Thus, if you start with too many products, you will not be able to do justice with any product, because you won't master any or all applications of any single product.

Thus, remember, the biggest principle which my marketing mentor taught me and It helps my everyday in my overall business that; LESS IS MORE.

Hope few examples gave you clarity over what I want you to understand. If you are thinking what should be the factors to choose the Right product are also very important to understand.

The Factors are

1. Your existing customer database
2. Your current customer's problem

3. Major application of each product line
4. Who is the customer, user, influencer in the Buying Process in your market
5. Market acceptance in terms of pricing
6. Market acceptance in terms of Product Choice like color preference, density, dimensions.

Thus to conclude, P for PRODUCT is one of the Major 4P's invented by Philip Kolter decades ago. The importance of choosing the right product will always stay important.

Hope you will choose the Right Product for your market and succeed.

Chapter 4

Choosing a Company Based on Price

Out of 100's of enquiries of the dealers who apply for dealership have a First ASK which they make over a first call is "share your price list".

I truly respect their action and I'm certain you and I also must have done the same many times in the buying decision in our lifetime. The difference which I want to get in your awareness is the fact that there the general one -time purchase decision can certainly be driven with pricing being at the first. However, in the long-term recurring association, pricing must be balanced with a lot of other attributes too.

The biggest mistake which a majority of dealers make is that they try to make an instant decision on the basis of Just the pricing. Price being an important P out of 4 P's of marketing plays a very vital role. However, pricing has to be balanced with a lot of other factors which need priority to succeed in long term.

Do you remember the bamboo story? It takes 5 years to deepen the roots underneath the earth level and when it grows,it grows exponentially. Thus, the choice which you have to make is to take a journey of bamboo or not.

I understand the fact the market dynamics demand the cheaper material, however, what you need to remember is one fact that good quality can be cheap..I remember the sayings of my mentor."Don't let cheapness come on the pathway to greatness."

In this last one decade, I experienced a few dealers who started working with us and left us after working for 2-4 years. When I took the feedback, I got to know that they shifted to cheaper segment material manufactured from unorganized players in the market. They think today that it was their right move. However, it is their lack of awareness of how it has hampered their long -term growth and market positioning in the lure of short- term profits for a few years.

The question which I would like to ask you is one and only, how " The choice of company purely based on pricing impacts your long term growth?"

When you associate with the price driven company, its core competency is to manufacture the low-cost products which compromises on quality. Their prime focus is to make their dealer competitive without even thinking that how the compromise done on quality will dent the functionality in the application. It eventually impacts the user, consumer, dealer in case of any dissatisfaction in the application. The consumer who had once negative experience due to any negligence has many side effects:

- It spoils the relationship with the dealer as he is front face for the consumer.
- The user (contractor | fabricator) who had some monetary setting with the dealer, initially also opts for a product in which he has maximum benefit. However, when any dysfunction happens due to poor quality product, then, he gets on back foot. This reduces his market value and referral rain which he could have got otherwise.
- It spoils the whole WPC industry as one negative customer experience spreads to 100s of those who haven't used the product.

Thus, one wrong decision of choosing the company and product based on price, impacts the whole business chain and every stakeholder involved in the game. You must be thinking: How can I operate smoothly in such a competitive market?

The solution which has worked best for a lot of my dealers is what I would like to present to you. They had a long term vision for this product | solution and could envision that they wanted to known as No. 1 Quality WPC specialist in their city(I will cover this Pointer in the coming chapter ahead).

They did one cutting edge strategy was that in front of entire good quality stocks, they also kept the poor quality.

Chapter 5

Product ko Samajh Dala, to Life Jheengalala

As per my understanding, there are 4 types of dealers which I have had a chance to work with in this last one decade. They are:

- The typical dealers who just stock the product, They believe that basic product technical understanding is enough for them to sell it in a big way.
- There is another set of dealers who go in-depth of product from all aspects and are also to justify the product Quality.
- The third category is those who understand product functionality and attributes and they have the tie up with the concerned fabricator also who can provide complete fabrication solution. Their agenda are clear. We need to serve the client with the complete solution.
- Then there is another set of dealers who have inhouse fabrication set up and they go guns in providing the complete end to end solution keeping a complete check on quality and product functioning in long run too.

Remember there is no right and wrong...The answer is its journey. You need to assess your current situation and where will you fit in today and what is that you desire to do and what does your market demands from you as a solution provider.

The mistake that lots of dealers make is they don't understand the depth of the product. The question that I want to ask you is: Whatever product you may be currently dealing in, how do you see that product?

With what lens do you see the product?

One of the mentors guided me, that seeing your product requires a similar kind of feeling which a mother has for a new- born baby. There need to be similar affection.

Technical understanding of the product is the most important aspect of any product.

I was speaking to a dealer and he asked me questions on product technicalities for which I also said. I need a couple of days to get that tested at our laboratory in the plant. Thus, when I Speak about the word Product Technicalities, it always reminds me of that dealer.

Technical depth and understanding its applications and what to use and where not developing a competency to distinguish the product based on measurement.

I know the basics. What's the need to go so deep and this is where majority of the dealers go wrong.

In fact, I would like to share a story which one of my mentors told me. He said that when he was working with a company manufacturing wall paneling and door opening solution products, they had a special initiative for every dealer they used to appoint. Every dealer post- appointment must visit to company plant along with their 1-2 contractors | carpenters. There was a complete training programme along with a factory visit, where every aspect like technical, mechanical, physical, functional, aesthetics are demonstrated. The contractor who accompanies the dealer feels super confident in every attribute of the product.

Now, you must be thinking that would it worth investing a day just for product understanding?.This return has given my handful of successful dealers 100 times return on their investment of time. You can count on it for the same. Your confidence to sell, demonstrate, differentiate will make your sales effortless. It means more sales and more profits making you authority in your city.

Chapter 6

Less Clarity on Ideal Customer

The shortest definition of marketing, my mentor guided me with shifted my being. The definition was "Market to Suno". YES. You read it right. To listen to market is the right path to sell faster.

If you want to sell and grow fast in your dealership business, then the question which must be arising in your mind would be:

What is the market you should focus on which will get you the fastest return?

Likewise, there is no right or wrong market, but certainly, the choice does exist between good or a better choice. Same way, on the path to grow fast, the selection of the right market is very very critical.

Now, when it comes to selecting the market, what does it mean? Likewise there are different levels of Truth. Same way, there are different layers to understand the Word Market.

When we talk about the market, it would be the target market, which would be a broader category like sub dealer network, architects, end customers, large scale private projects, Government projects, etc. Which one should you choose or which is right for you?

Answer in one word is "DEPENDS"

Thus, the clarity which I want to highlight is that there is no fixed answer for which there should be the right target market in your territory as it depends on a lot of other factors which you will surely get aware of after reading the whole book.

The fact that you need to understand is that a lot of dealers choose a product very wisely, however, when it comes to choosing the right target market,.that's where they make a choice which hampers their growth in the dealership of WPC.

Generally, they focus on more 2-3-4 or even more target markets. They attempt to choose the different types of target market and try to expand horizontally. The objective behind that is to tap the whole market and not leave anything over plate for others. I truly understand the feeling behind the same, however, let me walk you through the better process for the same.

The point to keep in mind is choosing the right 1 or 2 target markets like if you want to work with architects, then work with them. If you want to work with projects instead of building the sub dealer network, then it's absolutely fine. However, selecting and making the right choice in this context is very important. Principle of "Less is More" is applicable here also.

The next level of understanding which I want to introduce is that understanding the target market aone is not just enough. We need to go deeper in this concept of target market. You need to find the ideal client in your target market.

How to find the ideal client within the target market? If you learn this, it would be a million-dollar learning. My marketing mentor shared this with me and it has helped me hundreds of times, to make the right choice of our dealers. I will walk you through the entire process. This has benefited our dealers a lot to expand exponentially.

Your ideal client is the small specific set of customers who have common traits within that target market. Now what traits would serve as a baseline to identify that Ideal client?

The ideal client would be one who would give you 2 things for sure

- Profit and
- Respect to your values

As I said that it would be small specific set of customers, which means, that they would be a specific demographics and psychographics like

Architects in Chennai would be target market

Residential architects in Chennai can be an ideal client for Someone: But do remember, that they must give you Profit and resonate with your values.

Let's take another example: A dealer in Noida may have a target market to cover private projects. His ideal clients are the group housing builders who are good paymasters and Just Buy Product without involving in Installation.

It is just an example and I would like to say that identifying your ideal client profile is the Golden Key to Success.

You also need to remember that if you are still not clear with the ideal client and think that the counter footfall is your ideal client,then you need to rethink. Every client is not your ideal client. Thus, if you are starting afresh in WPC Sector or already working but not clear with the ideal client profile, then, you certainly need to hypothesize. It means you need to hypothesize to test a particular segment of market, listen to their voice. Understand their common patterns. Then test the hypothesis, validate the same and keep on improving the hypothesis.

Let's take an example: You assumed that I need to work with the residential architects in Chennai and get the product approved by them and you tested the same. However, after working with them, you realize that not all residential architects are your ideal clients. Those who make residential villa projects are your exact ideal client This is all you can understand by testing the market.

One more small mistake which I observed is that trying to the see the dealers who are already selling WPC and trying to copy their Selling Methodology.

The easiest way is to follow the footsteps as you don't need to reinvent the wheel. However, to get continual success, it requires efforts which are out of the box. It is said that the similar efforts done by the competitive dealers won't get them and you also the different results. The replication which majority of existing dealers when they make, they just see the product and then try to replicate the selling model of what others are doing.

If you are someone adding WPC to your kitty as a new product line. You may make this decision as seeing other dealers in the city or state are also selling WPC. The move is good. The details in this move are also mandatory to observe. For e.g.: you need to evaluate that those who are selling may be having a strong counter footfall. You need to see whether they are selling end to direct customers or direct consumer is coming through few carpenters. Remember this one liner: "The modalities change when the user and consumer changes."

Thus, while you understand a product line, an important factor to understand is to not to replicate the methodology of selling which others are doing.

Chapter 7

Intention to Sell or Solve a Problem

Whenever I speak to dealers across the country, the majority of them have a very strong pattern to sell and grab the business. I'm not denying the fact that selling should not be the end goal. However, there is an additional hidden layer which needs to be well understood for greater success in dealership business.

Let me Ask You one question: when any customer comes to you, then, does he just need the product because he needs the product or he is looking to solve a specific problem.

This is the Major Point. Every time you also buy something, if you analyze you are trying to solve a specific problem.

Let me explain by few examples:

- Buying a WPC Window Solution instead of Wooden Window Solution solve a specific problem of dampness, exterior weather issues and risk from attack of termite | Borer

- Buying a smart watch instead of a normal watch as it solves the problem to track the health
- Using Uber or Ola instead of owing the car and maintaining the car and driver solves the problem of movement at lesser cost and effort
- Using a wedding planner instead of choosing 20 vendors as it saves time and effort

The examples could be endless, but every buying decision made solves a specific pressing problem. The question which each one of us must ask that the sales happen much later than the origin and realization of the problem,then why is the primary focus purely on sales and not solving the pressing problem?

The answer which I have got to this question after speaking to several dealers do also vary like:

- Don't have that much time to understand the problem
- Don't have that sharp skill to ask the right questions to probe in a way which gets the customer to the perfect solution.
- Don't have bandwidth to solve the problem like if someone needs installation or on site services which can't be provided due to manpower or skill constraint.

Thus, the fact to realize is this that sales certainly increases exponentially if you invest time to probe the customer by asking the right question and get to the core pressing problem which the customer is trying to solve. The another side of the coin is when you solve the core problem in a most unique way which isn't being done by the competition.

An amazing example happened when a dealer called me and said that all the end customers in my city post their enquiry and when my sales person goes there, they ask for the samples. Their first question is who will take the measurements and who will install end to end ?

We crafted 3 irresistible offers to address this problem after profiling the customers in 3 categories :

1. The end user who are near the showroom, and want to feel the aesthetics of WPC products and understand functionality. The offer for them was to come to the showroom and our WPC experts will showcase a complete demonstration LIVE Which you won't get anywhere. If you have any concern on measurements and installation,we would take complete job end to end and deliver 100% satisfaction.
2. The end users who wanted to see samples and had their own local trusted fabricator. We offered them the courier of the same at a small cost of 1000 and said to them that this amount would be adjustable if you place us the final order.
3. The end user who wanted to see samples and clear that we don't want to search 3 to 5 vendors for

different works,they want one stop shop where they can get end to end solution and don't need to worry thereafter. For them, we crafted an offer that our WPC expert (Sales executive) will visit you and showcase the complete solution will get the measurements done of your site + will take over the complete installation with all necessary hardware.

The offer for them was we will charge Rs. 2000 and after its payment, the executive will come to your site and do the rest. This amount would also be adjustable.

Thus, solving a pressing problem of your customer in a unique way which needs to packed in an offer which is irresistible which customer feels stupid saying NO is the most crucial for your success which contributes to the success of the dealers.

However, an ironical part is that the majority of the dealers across India think that my business is purely selling the product. Thus, the complete focus is around selling the product and Journey ends there. I see this as an opportunity for ambitious dealer like you who wants to scale their business by doing something different which your competitors are not doing.

Your journey in sales never ends...once you have understood the problem, solve in a unique way, give them an offer, over deliver them than what you have committed, taking their feedback, getting the videos of their site, taking references from them. Then serving them. Thus, every customer a dot?? who will connect to you and help you to extend the line which will grow your business.

Chapter 8

Creating VALUE But Not Communicating

The Common ASK of dealers in the Building Material Industry when it comes to sales from a Product Company is " Will you provide a sales person?"

I would like to ask: what is the core job of that Salesperson?

You would say he would get you the sales and that's what any dealer of any product would want. But, if we get to the core of the point, how would sales happen by the Salesperson?

He would go to the cold prospects or the enquiries, find which one is more Interested and try his level best to close to grab the order. Thus, the core job is to generate leads and qualify them. However, his dependency stays on cold visits or cold leads or depends on Word of Mouth.

Thus, what happens is that the dealer gets a salesperson from the company, but, does it really work? Why it doesn't not work is because of 2-3 Reasons.

- The right person isn't appointed for the right work
- The person isn't clear about the strategy he is going to use for sales

- There is no strong review mechanism over that salesperson
- The person isn't trained enough with product and Sales Training Framework, that, he can convert enquiries with ease.

Now, the question is when a dealer should see his dealership business model, it's not advisable to completely depend on the salesperson for sales. Even if you get all the 4 things right, I'm certain, he won't stay for long (1-3 Years Max) in your territory for secondary sales generation. Now, what is the solution?

To understand this, you need to understand that keeping a person is not wrong, however, being entirely dependent on them for lead generation and qualification is not an advisable choice. That choice would increase the cost of operation as he would have to hit to 10 cold visits to find 1 right prospect. Thus, to maximize the ROI, the new methodology is to understand the game of lead generation. I call it **"Grahak Aapke Darwaze Tak."**

The point is How to Get the **"Grahak Aapke Darwaze Tak"**?

The lead engine of your business is lifeblood or oxygen of your business. This is the new approach. The point that must be coming in your mind right now must be: How to get those leads? Who will get it and from where will it come?

Let me relieve you by saying something which will be powerful for you in the context of lead generation. We at Ecoste, when we partner with any dealer, we see ourselves as a partner of Growth. That's where my role as a dealer growth specialist has helped many dealers to multifold their dealership business in less than 180 days. There are 2 primary ways through which you can do lead generation are:

- Online (Digital) Mediums
- Offline Mediums

Let me let you dive straight in the game of the same..I request you to understand with an open mind. There will be massive golden nuggets for you to grab and multiply your business. They aren't just learning which I have read or listened. These are tried and tested methods by several dealers across the country. I had a choice to just give you a glimpse in this chapter only but I wanted you to share a little in depth...Let's catch up in next chapter.

Chapter 9

Underestimating the Power of Lead Generation

Lead generation is the most the underestimated weapon by 99% of the dealers so far I have met across India. As explained in the previous chapter, I will be sharing not just learning which I have read or listened...These are tried and tested methods by several dealers across the country...The 2 methods would be

- Online Mediums
- Offline Mediums

In This digital era, every dealer has become so modernized. Every dealer uses all sorts of apps for booking cabs to order flowers and getting small grocery orders too. In B or C tier cities also, the exposure of each dealer is more or less equivalent to any dealer in metro cities too.

However, the area to be strengthened for the majority of the dealers across the country is to recall that the way they were adaptive to change themselves towards new technology for small things.Exactly the same way, they need to question themselves or yourself. Why not adapt in business for lead generation?

Thus, do leverage the most important weapon of this era: Digital Medium for growing your dealership business.. The digital medium could be based on what is your Ideal client profile. Let's take few examples:

If you are targeting consumers who are building their villa or a 4 storey building, then, targeting Facebook in your geographical territory would be great. You could also do Skip Ads in the local language in your territory, over Youtube and in that also you could run ads showing to a person who is showing interest in interior related videos or searching for a particular keyword on Youtube.

The quality of the leads which you would be getting would be great in this case as it would be hyper targeted.

If you are targeting interior designers or architects in your region, then, a great way to share the content on their specific groups over Facebook or by connecting them over Linkedin and sending good content. There are many techniques, but I'm just sharing only those which worked best for my dealers.

If you want to get more leads of end customers, then the best free way which has worked for a handful ambitious dealers will blow your Mind. It is not for everyone and it can only be implemented by highly ambitious dealers who want to do something long lasting. Not short term.

Just open Ecoste Kerala on Youtube. Let me walk you through the success story of our dealer in Kochi. They leveraged the power of Youtube as I already had done. He started making videos in the local language Malayalam. Today, they get more than 15 leads every day from Youtube. Now he's got the power to filter and choose the right prospect. If you really want to leverage your game using videos, I have a complete online course on nano videos..We can share the same with the selected Dealers who are truly ambitious to scale their game with next level authority.

If you are one of them, do, request us for the same. We will have a qualification call and post that we can share with you as a free gift from my side.

Now let's talk about the offline mediums. Thus, any medium which does not involves the digital medium as discussed prior is classified under offline medium. It must be popping in your head: which is the better one for me?

Answer again is DEPENDS. It depends on your Target Market and what does the ideal client wants to get communicated. I remember, a dealer from Satna, did something very amazing which blew away my mind. He wanted to target the local small residences which are new construction. To do that, it was difficult to spot on through Digital Medium unless they themselves go online and search to solve their problem. Thus, he decided to hire an electric loader for 300 Rs for 5 hours and then placed a complete door hanged with frame. There was a carpenter who went along with the driver and stopped at every new construction. They handed over a single leaflet and showcased them the solution. It created a great awareness in the market and everyone started him recognising as WPC expert in the city.

There are several other offline ways like tying-up with major contractors in the city and keeping good relationships with them by either gifting them or by helping them for their medical insurance or sponsoring their children education. This really makes them feel connected and gives them an opportunity to serve back by grabbing good orders and giving to the dealer.

Simple, you take care of them and they will take care of you.

Another important offline method is making contractors onboard with a small agreement. This one is done by one of my dealers in Raipur. He has made a certain number of good quality reliable contractors onboard. When I say onboard, it simply means if the dealer gets any particular customer order who wants an end to end solution, he refers to the contractor and get the job done. In this way, the contractor also gets a steady flow of contracts.

Another method was told by one of the dealers, who really got his foot right when the project construction began. He was from Punjab and he tied up with all the cement and TMT steel shops. He did put a small flex to advertise in their shop with a small miniature of door frame. The people came, asked about the product as it seemed to be a new product. The information started percolating to new construction site owners. It increased their sales.

Another method used by one of my punjab dealers that gave him phenomenal success was to place the flex board right outside the carpenter's shop. These carpenters generally have been spotted by the dealer and they are known ones. This really makes them feel special and feel obligated for the efforts done by the dealer and in turn, give the business back to the dealer.

Thus, there are several methods being online and offline for lead generation which will finally help to increase sales. The difference in 2 businesses which does lead generation and does not do lead generation is "Power of choosing the customers.' If you can have the power of choosing the customer rather than working with a handful of customers is always better.

However, just getting a lot of leads solves your Problem of sales?

The answer is: There is also something more in the game to grow your sales and profits. Let's dive in next chapter.

Chapter 10

Lead Conversion is the Another Side of Coin

Lead generation is one side of the coin. When the lead comes, it gets qualified and it gets converted or lost. Thus, the other side of the coin is conversion of the leads. Thus, there are several factors which certainly impacts the conversion. It would get categorized in 2 segments

- Quality Impacts Conversion
- Quantity Impacts Conversion

Quality Impacts Conversion: What quality am I talking about? In Quality Aspect, there are few major pointers which must be kept in mind which hit your conversion:

- How fast your inquiry gets addressed? Which means when someone calls or visits, how fast does the enquiry problem get dressed and he gets the solution he/she is looking for?
- Who is the first point of contact? Which means who addresses the enquiry at the first attempt and what Information is being taken? What is the conviction level when the inquiry is being addressed?

- Is the enquiry being sold or being served? Which means is he just being pushed for the product the dealer has or is the problem of the customer being understood and being served with the right solution?
- Is the customer being offered with an irresistible offer, after listening customer feels stupid saying NO? Which means the customer is being offered with an offer which solves the problem of the customer which is unique from your competition.
- Is the value force which your customer feels is more than the cost force? Which means the value force which your customer gets must be the total cost the customer expends..
- How the customer being showcased with the solution which increases his conviction for the new product? Which means when a customer comes to showroom, is he getting a complete view of the application or just getting glimpse of raw samples?

Quantity Impacts Conversion

When it comes to quantity, It simply means review of numbers and Review of Reports at a Set Frequency. This in itself requires not just a specific skill set but also the mindset. This simply means that, even if you have enough leads and have a good team to convert the same,BUT if you're not reviewing the numbers and reports, then be sure you are losing something big on something. This does involve lot of important pointers which are under mentioned:

- Is the data of all enquiries with few essential questions being stored somewhere in an excel sheet or a CRM Software, so that the follow ups can be done at the right time?
- Is the data getting in a right shape of a report which can be easily viewed, so that the right question can be asked and right decision can be made?
- Once the report takes shape, is it being updated on a daily basis and being reviewed and monitored so that no enquiry is being left out which'll certainly increase your conversion.

Certainly, when it comes to the game of conversion, there are many other impacting pointers which have helped my lot of dealers to become No. 1 dealer in their respective cities. The main fundamental can be well explained using a trust value graph.

Let me ask you a question?

Recall your last 3 buying decisions. And How did you take that decision? If you would observe, you would feel that, you must have bought from someone whom you had more trust.

The next question arises: How did you develop that trust?..Simple. Someone who may have added an extra layer of efforts to guide you making your research cheaper, better and faster. Correct?

Or, someone who was able to reduce your Cost Force and increase Value Force...For eg: You wanted to buy a new car and instead of you visiting showroom, you left an inquiry and someone called you and asked a preferred slot and arranged a test drive for you explaining the features and benefits by a technical person. Now, you have formed a decision, that you are getting good value over the cost for the car you are expending.

Can you correlate that this is how you make any buying decision?

Whenever you or your customer makes any buying decision, the cost force has to go down. Now, you must be thinking how can you reduce its cost force and increase value force?

Let me Share few reasons how you can do that which I learnt from Jim Edwards in his copywriting Secrets:

1). Make People Money

2). Save Money

3). Reduce Efforts

4). Reduce Mental and Physical pain

5). Increase Reputation

Now, what does the Trust Value Graph simply mean?

It simply means that if you operate in the fourth spectrum, which is of high value and high trust, it's the best zone to operate.

It is simply because you are creating value more than your customer expects and trust as a by-product is getting created automatically.

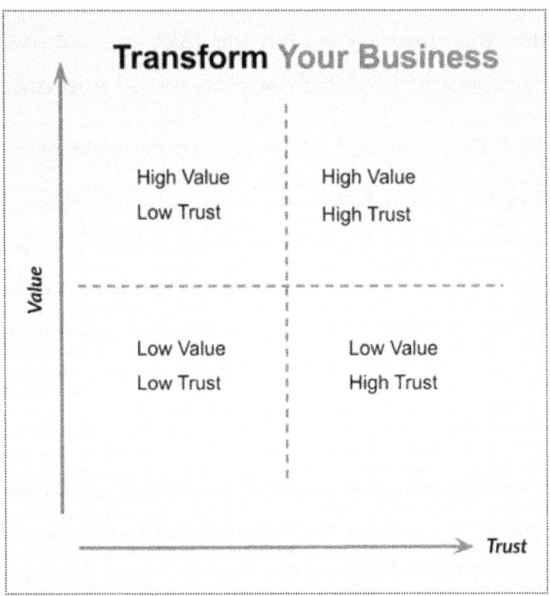

However, the biggest mistake which is most common amongst every dealer in BMC industry is that even if dealer is offering good services, they don't present the same in a form of an offer because of which the customer is not able to perceive the value which he desires.

Let me explain: 2 Vendors Approach to a Single inquiry for door opening solution..let's see the difference.

Vendor an offer: I have WPC door opening and these are its features and benefits and this is its price.

Vendor B Offer: We are WPC Solution Experts and we can offer you free demonstration with complete working at our Showroom and that is possible virtually and physically. If you want our executive to get the miniature sample, then, that is also possible for which we take a commitment fees of 1K which would be 100% adjustable of you order us.

Not just this, we will offer you free measurements, free color guidance, complete end to end installation from our experts ensuring the Quality at every step. You don't need to go to any vendor for anything after choosing us and all this installation be done in 48 hours over a weekend so that you don't have to miss your work (As the door opening solution will come as pre-ready solution to your site),

Now, get into the shoes of the customer and think, which vendor would you choose. You would get the answer.

Would you not willing to pay 5-10% extra easily given that the offer solves your problem and offer you more value than the Cost (Financial + Physical + Mental).

Another mistake is creating value,but not communicating value.

Let me explain...your offer is like vendor B and is too Good for someone who is looking to get his problem solved. BUT, you as solution provider, have the offer but you aren't showcasing to enough number of people who are looking for it.

You must be thinking now, if we increase the leads, then I can showcase the same offer to enough leads. Isn't it?

Yes you can...BUT, there is one clarity..This also has 2 Step approach which few of my success stories who adopted, got the 200% or more growth in their Sales and Profits.

Let me take you to a time in 2015 when it was just 2 years when I launched WPC in Indian Market and I was struggling to sell as education of the product was very low to everyone...

The best thing which helped me over this course of period was communicating value through the free videos which we created on Youtube. Today,our channel Ecoste, is Number One Global Channel with over 1 lac subscribers and more than 15 million views.

Not to brag, but, what helped me was communicating value before the customer thinks at a nascent stage of solving a problem.

Thus, you have created a great offer and now you have leads to communicate also. This is also very good BUT a better approach which you must implement is..."Create and communicate value much before your customer even thinks of buying and do over deliver than what he desires."

And the best medium which has really worked best for me and my dealer which made them authority and sell at a premium than their competitors is "Communicating value through the videos over Youtube."

The success mantra for one of my dealers was that he created videos in Malayalam for Kerala market. This really gave them the boost as people could relate so much. They were able to create value in local language and trust was a by- product...It certainly helped them to sell in bulk easily.

In this journey, creating a small video of your success really helps. Like videos of live installation, feedback of customer....and upload on Youtube Channel..Showcase to the inquires when they have any doubt.

Fore. g. : Someone who doubts about the screw holding... showcase a video of someone who got the work done 4 years and facing no issues. This would really reduce your efforts to strip the objection of screw holding and sales will happen fast and easy.

Chapter 11

Mindset in the Key

This chapter should have been first as it is most important but there is a reason why I am sharing it at the end. Out of all the dealers, I have got an opportunity to work with, I observed one thing in common. Those who got fast and consistent success, were the ones who realized that the power of mindset is as important as the skills they are learning for their business growth.

Please don't get offended by understanding that there is a problem with the mindset of dealers. In fact, they have much better business sense than me. However, I see much potential for ambitious dealers, if they really understand the power of mindset and leverage its true power.

You must have read that in business it's 80% Mindset Game and 20% skill set. Thus, this chapter holds a great significance.

WHY?

Simply because , if I mentor you 1-2-1 and guide with all the learning of my successful dealers...Still...if you aren't ready, with your Mindset, trust me,It will just be knowledge which would increase your confidence in the t beginning, but it won't help you to really implement and grow your dealership business in the long run.

Mindset is such a vast topic that I would certainly like to write a separate book about it in the near future. However, let me simplify the same in easy words for you.

Mindset has several layers like an onion which has to be peeled and it will make sense in a beautiful way to you..

- What are you doing?
- Why are you doing ?
- How Are you doing?
- Are you happy doing what you want to Do and Enjoying the game to the fullest?
- How Are your thoughts, words and actions which you speak to yourself and others about your business
- How are your thoughts, words which you speak to yourself about you?
- Are your actions aligned to what you think and speak about yourself?
- Are your habits in sync with your goals?
- What is your short term and long term vision and are your actions aligned to the same?
- Are your personality traits aligned to achieve the goals for your business?

- How strong are you to handle the challenges?

Mindset which impacts your Business has 5 Pillars which are mentioned below:

1. **What you Think about you and your Business:** That is the starting point. It is not the stories of your failures which you may have faced in the journey of your success. It is how you see yourself first in the game you are playing?

   When I say what you think about you? It simply means what perception or self-image you hold about yourself....If you hold a strong self-image about what kind of visionary dealer you are.....It doesn't just mean where you are right now...but how strongly you hold an image of yourself of where you want to go.

   Remember: you would manifest what you are and not what you want. Let's say you want to make 15 Lacs of Profit, but if your self-image or self-worth to earn that much amount does not become a true part of your identity,you will feel that I desperately want success, but not able to grab. Its simple reason is that low self -image doesn't allow you to be worthy of the success you want...So, keep thinking yourself worthy of the goal You want to accomplish is the key.

2. **Habits:** Your habits for calibration in finance, health and relationship creating a harmonious balance:

"Habits Make or Break your Life". The habits in all 3 areas of your life need to be defined and measured in simple words.

a. **Health:** What you do to maintain your health as a part of habit and are you tracking on a simple sheet? How many days a week and month you do any form of physical exercise and the healthy food you consume? You may think, how will it impact my business. The answer is, your business is a direct reflection of your being. Once you exercise, you release all toxic energies. Your mind becomes silent, clean to make business decisions sharper and faster.

b. **Relationships:** The relationships directly shape the levels of joy and peace in your overall being which directly prepares you how calmly you do business. Your healthy relationships with everyone at home and family is the key to makingyou a more stable and sharp entrepreneur.

c. **Finance:** How you manage your finances truly decides the wealth you make. Do you have few required reports at right intervals, which are prepared by your accountant and reviewed by you? Fore. g.; Debtor's Ageing,Debtors' Follow up response, Creditors' Ageing, Cash Flow in Business, Monthly Balance Sheet, P&L, Daily Stock Analysis, Reorder Levels so on and so forth These reports must be seen by dealer at the right intervals and decisions must be based on data as a habit to create wealth.

3. **Aim and Effort in calibration of short term and Long term Goal:** The biggest mistake after speaking to a lot of dealers is misalignment between aim and effort..Once an aim is set, its efforts are plotted and they need to be aligned in short and long run. However, in the beginning, the efforts are aligned to the aim, but after a while, the efforts do not seem to be aligned to the aim. This pattern of observing daily by just asking yourself a single question " Are my efforts aligned to my aim?"

   Why does it Happen? It's because the monkey mind wanders and deviates easily the efforts which aren't in coherence with the aim.

4. **Coachable:** Everything begins with: How coachable and receptive you are for learning new things which are required to upscale your game? The only reason why I work with ambitious dealers is that they have a zeal to grow the business by learning what I say to them after my years of experience.

   The main attribute which is required to grow to understand that to grow the dealership business, there are certain requisite skills which are required. Once a gap analysis is done, it becomes very easy provided you are receptive to mentoring.

5. **Mindset for Making it Process Driven than People Driven:** Do you feel that your dealership business is too much person driven and someone leaves the business, your business operation gets in fire fighting mode. All these lead to the involvement of the time of the most precious person in the organization which is business owner.

   Have you ever calculated the per hour cost of your time? Have you assessed what if you delegate the work which you do and is not necessary for you to do ? The crux is, the most important resource in the organization does those works which do not necessarily lead to business growth.

   Moreover, I want to ask you what if you make a lot of money but you don't have time for yourself and your family. You lose your work -life balance... Right?

   Thus, the methodology which helps a dealer is to see your dealership business from a long-term perspective. It simply means, it's important to have the right people doing the right job with the right process.

6. **Mindset to Surround yourself with what People:** It's said that you are an average of 5 People you surround yourself with. Thus, a mindset to stay with people who have great intellect, are ambitious, sharp in business, has diverse skill sets, will certainly help you grow effortlessly in your dealership business.

Concluding Chapter

After reading all these Chapters, you must be very clear with whatever stage you are at, whether starting WPC as a fresh product line or wish to rework on the strategy of selling WPC in the most differentiated way in the market. This will certainly make you an authority. No. 1 WPC solution dealer in your city for sure.

I want to ask, do you still feel that competition is the problem? Pls read the line which I refer from an online meeting which I do for 200% dealer growth every month.

So...Do You Agree?

Is competition the problem?

Its is that we are still using the same sales & marketing **style which has its reduced effectiveness over the years...** It's time to upgrade the way you do marketing & selling.

The crux is that I have shared everything possible I have learned over the platter & now you have 2 choices:

- **Choice 1:** To implement yourself and face the grind yourself to succeed fast.
- **Choice 2:** To have me By Your side to handhold You to Become a No 1 WPC Expert in Your city & start making 3-10 Lacs of Monthly Profit selling effortlessly.

If Others can...Why Can't You...Trust yourself & Just Submit your application of Interest...Since we Make Very Less Number of new Partners each Quarter because we don't just believe in creating them but also nurturing them....Thus, the slots would be limited...Apply for the Slot & Let's speak over a 1-2-1 session for 15 Min after we receive all your details:

QR; 

In case Qr is not Accessible, then Email Your Name, Mobile Details at contact@ecoste.in

YoutubeChannel: Type Ecoste on YouTube & Don't forget to Subscribe.

Website: www.ecoste.in

Do Watch Our YoutubeChannel: Type Ecoste on YouTube & Don't forget to Subscribe.

www.ingramcontent.com/pod-product-compliance
Ingram Content Group UK Ltd.
Pitfield, Milton Keynes, MK11 3LW, UK
UKHW021655190726
13853UKWH00001B/266